EONS

ht fast and direct
; regular wing-
t; noisy on take-
large body, small
d evident in flight

GULLS

Powerful, direct flight
with slow wingbeats
alternates with glid-
ing, hovering and
wheeling; wings nar-
row, long and fairly
pointed

OWLS

Flight absolutely si-
lent; irregular, flap-
ping wing action on
broad, round-tipped
wings; blunt head,
short tail evident in
flight

HAWKS

Rounded, broad
wings give fast, agile
flight; capable of
soaring and gliding;
short neck, long tail
evident in flight

RKS

ht vigorous, on
ad-based, tapered
gs; rises vertically
ing; hovers at
siderable height;
ps directly or in
al

VEN

ight wings with
gered' primaries,
verful flight with
ady wingbeat;
able of spectac-
aerobatics, large
d and beak

FALCONS

Broad-based wings
tapering to a long
point; very fast flight,
rapid wingbeat;
glides, dives and
(kestrel) hovers

Series 536

Children and adults who wish to identify more positively the birds they see in woods, hedgerows and heathland, will find John Leigh-Pemberton's superb illustrations most helpful. These – and the clear, interesting and reliable text – will doubtless stimulate many people to take an even greater interest in bird life.

HEATH and WOODLAND BIRDS

by
JOHN LEIGH-PEMBERTON

Ladybird Books Ltd Loughborough

Capercaillie *(cock above, hen below)*

The Capercaillie is our largest game-bird and is a resident in parts of Scotland. Two hundred years ago it became extinct in Britain, but was re-introduced in 1837 by importing birds from Scandinavia.

This is a woodland bird, breeding only among pine trees, the cock being very much larger than the hen and very different in plumage. Although so big, the Capercaillie is surprisingly agile when flying among trees, and spends much time perched in them. Food consists almost entirely of the young shoots of trees, particularly pine and larch, but during the breeding season the hen and young birds also eat insects and grubs.

The nest is usually a hollow, scraped by the hen among vegetation at the foot of a tree. There is one brood of between five and eight eggs, and as these are laid, the hen adds lining material to the nest. The cock takes no part in hatching or tending the young, which can fly at about three weeks old.

The hen has a harsh 'kok-kok' call, but the cock is usually silent except in the breeding season when he utters the most astonishing 'song' – a mixture which starts with a tapping sound, followed by a noise like drawing a cork and ending with a sound like grinding a knife.

Black Grouse *(hen above, cock below)*

This is a large resident bird, once much more numerous than it is now, and found in a few localities such as Exmoor, Wales, northern England and Scotland. Its territory is the edge of moorland and woodland, not always on high ground but always among trees and bushes.

The Blackcock and the Greyhen (as the female is called) are very different in plumage. The lyre-shaped tail of the cock is spread like a fan during the courtship display in the spring, when 'packs' of from ten to twenty birds gather at special patches of ground called 'leks'. Here, often as early as January and sometimes again in the autumn, the cocks display and fight, uttering a mixture of noises from hissing and bubbling to cooing and crowing.

Food consists almost entirely of the tender shoots of trees, but beetles and other insects are eaten in the spring and autumn, and wild berries, fruit and seeds in season. Nesting takes place in mid-May, a single brood being raised from between six and ten eggs. The eggs are laid on the ground in a hollow among grass or heather, although sometimes Black Grouse will nest in a tree in the old nest of some other bird. Incubation of the eggs takes about twenty-six days, and hatching and brooding the chicks is by the hen only.

Red Grouse *(below: hen left, cock right)*
Ring Ouzel *(above: hen left, cock right)*

The Red Grouse is a resident moorland bird found throughout Scotland and in parts of Wales, northern England and Exmoor. Another very similar race of Grouse is found in Ireland.

In autumn, Grouse form in 'packs' and visit lower-lying agricultural land to feed among stubble. Adult birds feed almost entirely on vegetable matter, such as young shoots and flowers of heather, and on crow-berries. The chicks feed chiefly on insects. The principal cry is the characteristic crow of the cock bird – 'go-back go-back-back-back-back'. The nest, a hollow on the ground, is often among heather, and from six to eleven eggs, in a single brood, are incubated by the hen alone. The young birds fly in about twelve days.

Another moorland bird is the Ring Ouzel, a summer visitor breeding in Scotland, Wales and in parts of England and Ireland. Some birds stay through the winter. The nest is rather like that of a Blackbird*, but is built on a foundation of heather and placed on a bank, in a bush, or even on an old building. There are usually two broods of four eggs which, incubated by both parents, hatch in fourteen days.

Ring Ouzels have a piping but monotonous song, with call and alarm notes rather like those of the closely related Blackbird. Their food consists of berries and seeds, in addition to small worms and insects.

See 'Garden Birds'

Ptarmigan *(summer plumage above, autumn centre;*
winter plumage below; hen left, cock right)

Ptarmigan are inhabitants of the high mountains of northern Scotland and of some of the Western Isles. This is a resident bird, a relative of the Red Grouse, found only above two thousand feet. It is an even stronger flyer than the Red Grouse, rapid wing beats alternating with long glides on which it can climb or dive.

The cry of the Ptarmigan is a hoarse croak, or a continuous 'crackling' noise. Of most interest, perhaps, is the beautiful plumage upon which the bird relies for camouflage as it crouches, hardly visible, among rocks and scant vegetation. This plumage, blackish brown in spring and summer, turns to grey in autumn and, except for black tail feathers, to pure white in winter.

Even at high altitudes the nest is no more than a hollow on the ground, sheltered by rock and sometimes thinly-lined with grass by the hen as egg laying progresses. Two hens sometimes lay in the same nest, but the usual clutch is from five to nine eggs, hatched in about twenty-five days by the hen alone. There is only one brood, which is guarded by the cock. The chicks, which have little feathered feet, can fly in about ten days.

Food consists of shoots, leaves and berries, with a few insects, particularly craneflies. In winter Ptarmigan will burrow into a snowdrift to obtain food.

Common Partridge *(below)*
Red-Legged, or 'French' Partridge *(above)*

The Common Partridge is a resident bird, distributed throughout England and Wales, but more locally in Scotland. It inhabits agricultural land and, chiefly because of the changes in modern farming methods, it is becoming scarcer. It is a strong, fast flyer and has always been popular as a game-bird. Its call is a loud, harsh 'kee-wit kee-wit-it-it', and its food consists of fruit, grain and weed seeds as well as insects.

The nest is a hollow, lined with grass and hidden among rough ground cover or under a hedge. From nine to twenty eggs, in a single brood, are hatched by the hen alone. Like most game-birds, the chicks quickly become independent and can fly in about sixteen days.

The slightly larger Red-legged Partridge is a resident too, introduced from France in 1770, and occupying the same type of country as the Common Partridge as well as downland, marshes and even coastal shingle. Its food is similar, and like the Common Partridge it flies in parties called 'coveys', but it is more reluctant to fly and prefers to run. Nests, lined with grass and feathers, are on the ground under cover, and sometimes two simultaneous clutches of about ten eggs each are laid, one being incubated by the hen and the other by the cock.

The usual cry is a loud 'chucka-chucka'.

Pheasant *(cock above, hen below)*

The Pheasant, a big, resident bird found throughout almost the whole of Britain, was originally introduced here from Asia Minor – possibly more than a thousand years ago. Since then, many other sorts of Pheasants have been imported – notably Chinese (which have a white collar), and Japanese and Mongolian birds of varying plumage. All these have interbred, so that now no pure-bred Pheasants exist here.

Pheasants like woodland and farmland, and in many places are preserved specially for shooting. They fly straight and fast for a short distance and then glide down to cover. They prefer to live on the ground, although they generally roost in trees at night. From eight to fifteen eggs are laid on the ground in a roughly-lined nest under cover. Incubation is usually by the hen only, and the chicks, which can fly in about fourteen days, are fed by the hen alone. There is only one brood. Food is very varied – from seeds, fruit and berries to beetles, grubs, snails and even mice.

The usual cry, or crow, of the cock Pheasant is a familiar country sound – 'korrk-kor-karrk' – although this varies slightly. The hen gives a weak whistling cry when alarmed.

Other ornamental Pheasants have been introduced into parks and aviaries – Golden, Reeve's and Lady Amherst's Pheasants in particular. These often escape and live in the wild state.

Woodcock *(above)*
Corncrake *(below)*

In wooded areas over most of Britain, the Woodcock is a resident. In winter some birds migrate to Ireland and the Continent, while others arrive here. Woodcock live chiefly on earthworms, but also eat other insects and some vegetable matter. Feeding takes place at dusk, the Woodcock spending the day in cover. The rather variable flight is notable for a special display, called 'roding', at breeding time, the male flying with slow wing beats in a circle and uttering two distinct notes – 'kroho' and 'chizzic'.

Four eggs are laid, often in moss at the foot of a tree. Sometimes there are two broods, incubated and raised by the hen alone. Woodcock will carry their young from place to place, flying with them held between their thighs.

The Corncrake is a summer visitor, becoming rarer but fairly frequent in Scotland and northern England. It inhabits grassland and, except at dusk and dawn, spends much of its life concealed. Its note, a continuously repeated 'rerp-rerp', is often the only clue to its presence.

The nest is in thick grass and from eight to twelve eggs are laid, hatched by the hen alone. The young leave the nest very early, but cannot fly until the thirty-fourth day. Food consists mostly of various insects, with small amounts of grass and weeds.

Turtle Dove *(above)*
Stock Dove *(below)*

The Turtle Dove frequents cultivated ground with thin woodland and hedgerows. This summer visitor (chiefly to southern England) is easily recognised by its small size, long black and white tail and chestnut back, and by its distinctive, pleasing note – 'turr-turr'. Its flight is similar to that of other pigeons, but with more rapid wing beats. The seeds of weeds and a few leaves are the chief items of diet, and it does less damage to crops than other doves.

The nest, usually placed in a tall bush or thorn tree, is a flimsy structure of small twigs, often without any sort of lining. There are two eggs incubated by both parents, and two broods are normal.

The somewhat larger Stock Dove is a resident, in many ways very like the Woodpigeon*, but it can be found on cliffs and sand dunes as well as woodland and farmland. Being less abundant than the Wood-pigeon, it probably does less damage, although its food is similar. It is commoner in the south than in the north of Britain. The 'coo' is not as musical as that of most doves – a gruff 'oo-oof'. Like most pigeons and doves it tends to nest in colonies, but in a hollow tree or rabbit burrow and not often among branches. There are usually two broods of two eggs, both parents incubating and feeding the chicks, or 'squabs', as the young of pigeons are called.

Cuckoo *(above)*
Meadow Pipit *(below)*

The Cuckoo, a summer visitor to all parts of Britain, arrives in late March and leaves in August and September. The familiar note 'cuck-coo' can be heard until the end of June, and the bird can be further recognised by its long tail and rapid wing beats. It feeds chiefly on insects.

The Cuckoo is most notable for its method of breeding. It builds no nest of its own but lays in the nest of some other bird, removing one of the host's eggs, which it usually eats. The Cuckoo's egg often resembles the host's eggs, and is reared by the host. It hatches quicker than the eggs of most other birds, (about twelve days), and after hatching the young Cuckoo pushes other eggs or chicks out of the nest. A hen Cuckoo lays about twenty eggs a season in this way.

A frequent host of the Cuckoo is the Meadow Pipit. This is a resident, insect-eating bird which breeds on pastures or moorland, building on the ground a well-made nest lined with grass and hair. Four or five eggs are laid, incubated by the hen for about fourteen days; the young are fed by both parents.

This member of the Wagtail family has a rather weak, trilling song, uttered as it rises in flight and finishing with a final trill as it glides down.

Yellow Wagtail *(above)*
Grey Wagtail *(below: hen above, cock below)*

Although Wagtails like to live near water, the Yellow Wagtail, most commonly found in England and Wales, also frequents open heath or moorland. This is a summer visitor which breeds here, nesting on the ground where there is thick cover, and producing two broods of five or six eggs. The nest is recognisable by its very thick lining of hair, and both parents incubate the eggs and feed the young.

The chief song is a warble, rather like that of a Robin*, but usually delivered in flight. There is also a drawn-out call note – 'tseeep'. The hen, not shown, has slightly duller plumage than the male.

Grey Wagtails are resident birds, usually found in hilly districts and almost always seen near water, particularly running streams, close to which they quite often rest in a crevice or among the roots of trees. Apart from the colouring, they are conspicuous by the length of tail which is constantly flicked up and down. The usual note is a sharp 'tsiz-it', and the song, not often heard, is a short warble 'zee-zee-zee-zee'. From four to six eggs are laid in a nest made from a variety of materials, and incubation and tending the young is by both parents. There are sometimes two broods and, like other Wagtails, the young can fly in about twelve days.

Both species are mainly insect eaters.

Skylark (above)

Yellowhammer (below: cock above, hen below).

The Skylark is with us throughout the year although in autumn large flocks of birds bred here leave us, while others from the continent take their place. Skylarks frequent open grassland from sea level to high moorland, being absent from wooded country and steep valleys. They nest on the ground, building a nest of grass and a little hair in a hollow or among crops. Usually there are three or four eggs, hatched by the hen; the young are fed by both parents. Food is mainly vegetable – seeds, young plants and clover, but a few earthworms and insects are also eaten.

This little bird produces, throughout almost the whole year, the most beautiful, vigorous song – a long succession of musical phrases, delivered as the bird ascends in vertical flight, as it hovers, often at a considerable height, and as it floats down.

Yellowhammers frequent grassy country with plenty of cover, such as hedgerows. They are resident birds, generally distributed over most of Britain. They have a short call-note – 'chink', and a song which is said to sound like the phrase – 'little-bit-of-bread-and-no-cheese'. Although they eat a few insects, the largest part of their diet consists of all sorts of seeds and fruits.

Three or four eggs are laid in a hair-lined nest built of grass and moss, usually on the ground among cover.

Rook *(above)*
Hooded Crow *(below)*

These are large resident members of the Crow family, highly intelligent birds which eat a great variety of foods, from carrion and animal matter to seeds and berries. Both build sturdy nests of twigs and sticks, bound together with earth. These are lined with wool and hair in the case of the Hooded Crow, and with grass and leaves in the case of the Rook. Nests are usually in a tree, but can be in a fairly low bush, and the Hooded Crow may build on a cliff-face while Rooks occasionally nest on a building.

The Hooded Crow is a solitary bird found in Ireland, the Isle of Man and Scotland, where it overlaps the range of the Carrion Crow*, with which it will inter-breed and to which it is in many ways very similar. It raises a single brood from four to six eggs.

The Rook, distinguishable by its bare face, lives in large colonies. Groups of nests are built among the upper branches of trees; these are known as 'rookeries', many of them being long-established and nearly always close to farms or villages, but not in built-up areas. Here, throughout the year, the Rook's familiar 'caw' or 'kaar' can be heard, as well as other calls perhaps in imitation of other birds such as gulls. Rooks raise a single brood from three to five eggs.

Jackdaw *(above)*
Raven *(below)*

The Jackdaw is our smallest Crow, found in areas ranging from towns to the wildest of coastal cliffs. A sociable, jaunty bird, it spends much time strutting about on the ground, although it is an extremely skilful flyer. Like all crows, it has a trick of hiding food and other objects. It is also a clever mimic. Two calls – 'kyow' and a sharp – 'jack' – are characteristic.

Colonies of Jackdaws nest in holes in old trees, on a cliff, or among ruins. Occasionally they build deep nests in trees, or occupy old Rooks' nests. Four to six eggs are usual, laid in a nest made of sticks and lined with hair and wool. There is one brood, and the young birds do not fly until they are about a month old.

The Raven is our largest Crow. A resident, it is found in hilly parts of Britain or in woodland or coastal areas. It is a remarkable flyer, performing aerobatics (including a 'roll') during the breeding season. The principal call is a deep, barking 'pruk-pruk', but many other cries are used. It will eat anything from quite large animals and fish to vegetable matter.

Ravens lay from four to six eggs in a nest built of sticks, heather and earth, well-lined with wool and leaves. The young hatch in twenty-one days, but it is about six weeks before they can fly.

Fieldfare *(above)*
Waxwing *(below)*

These two birds are winter visitors to Britain, and neither of them breed here. The Fieldfare, coming from northern Europe, is the larger and commoner of the two, and can be found, chiefly on farmland, between October and April in most parts of Britain. This is a gregarious bird – that is one that goes about in flocks, often in company with Redwings*. In flight it· utters a harsh 'cha-cha-chack', often in chorus as the flock moves restlessly about in search of food. This consists of slugs, insects and berries.

In many respects, such as stance and flight, it resembles its relative, the Mistle Thrush*.

The Waxwing is a more uncommon bird, a few coming here every winter from Finland and Russia. In some years, when food is scarce in its own country, it appears here in some numbers, but usually on the east side of Britain; it is rare in Wales and northern Scotland.

It derives its name from the curious wax-like tips to the secondary wing feathers – the colour and texture of sealing wax.

Waxwings appear in small parties, perching on any tree which has berries – their principal food. They are stolid, rather tame birds, quite likely to be seen in gardens as well as open country and fir plantations. The usual note is a high-pitched, rather feeble trill, like that of a Tit*.

Stonechat (above: cock above, hen below)

Firecrest (below)

Heaths, or downland near the sea, are the most
likely places to see Stonechats. They are resident
birds, but only found in certain parts of Britain, and
are becoming scarcer.

This handsome little bird, a member of the Thrush
family, has a song somewhat like that of the Dunnock*,
and this it sings in ascending flight or when perched
prominently on a bush. The usual call-note is a metallic
'chat-chat'. Insects and earthworms form the greatest
part of its diet. Two broods of five or six eggs are normal,
laid in a nest of grass, moss, hair and a few feathers.
This is on the ground, or close to it in a bush, and is
built by the hen alone.

Another rare bird is the tiny Firecrest, an autumn
visitor in small numbers mostly to East Anglia and
the coastal districts of southern England. It is very
similar to our own resident Goldcrest (*page 46*), but
has a well-marked white stripe above the eye and a dark
line through it; its crest tends to be redder and it is
less confined to fir plantations, being at home among
low cover such as bracken.

Less than four inches long, the Firecrest is a member
of the Kinglet family, coming to us from Denmark
and central Europe. Some winter here and a few sometimes appear in spring.

Whinchat *(top: hen above, cock below)*
Nightjar *(below)*

The smart little Whinchat is another member of the Thrush family, and is a summer visitor which breeds here in certain areas. It is commonest in Wales, northern England and Scotland, preferring country with rough grassland and scattered bushes. It does not hide in cover, as many small birds do, but perches boldly in the open. Its song is similar to, but less musical than that of the Stonechat (*page 32*). It feeds almost entirely on insects.

Five or six bright bluish-green eggs are laid in a nest built among long grass and formed of grass and moss with a lining of fine grass and hair. The hen builds the nest and incubates the eggs, but the cock helps to feed the chicks. As a rule there are two broods.

The Nightjar, a summer visitor, is a bird seen mostly at dusk when it is active, with a swallow-like flight, in chasing and catching in the air the various insects upon which it lives. During the day it rests, lying flat along a branch, but it can be heard at night uttering in flights its soft 'coo-ic' call. The song is a curious 'churring' sound, and there is also a clapping noise made by beating the wings together over the back.

Nightjars, which have huge mouths but tiny beaks, nest on the bare ground and normally lay two eggs. There are two broods.

Wheatear *(top: cock above, hen below)*

Lapwing *(below and in flight)*

The Wheatear is a summer visitor, which breeds here on downland and upland pastures. Although it perches on fences and likes to sing from a rock or hillock, it spends much time on the ground. Food consists of spiders and insects which it catches in the air, making short fluttering flights from the ground to do so. In similar flights it sings a vigorous song not unlike that of the Skylark (*page 24*).

The nest is a hole in the ground or among rocks, and both cock and hen build the nest and feed the young. Incubation of the six eggs is by the hen alone. There is normally only one brood.

The Lapwing, the commonest of our resident waders, is found not only on mudflats and marshes but also on cultivated land and moorland. Out of the breeding season it is usually seen in large flocks, and in the autumn further flocks arrive from the Continent, while some home-bred birds migrate to Spain and Ireland. Food consists mostly of earthworms, but includes insects and some vegetable matter.

The cry of the Lapwing is the familiar 'pee-wit' – an alternative name for the bird – and the breeding song, uttered in aerobatic flight, is an elaboration of this. The nest, usually containing four eggs, is on the ground, a muddy hollow lined with grass and slightly raised. Another name for this bird is – the Green Plover.

Woodlark (top)
Redstart (below: cock left, hen right)

Rough grassland with scattered trees, or the edges of woods, preferably on sandy soil, are the sort of areas favoured by the Woodlark. Very similar to the Skylark, but smaller and with a shorter tail, this bird is a resident, chiefly in southern England. The Woodlark's song, often heard at night, is sweeter but less vigorous; in flight it soars less high but flies, singing, in wide circles.

The neat, small nest is built on the ground, made of grass, moss and hair, usually in a sheltered hollow but sometimes quite exposed. There are two broods of three or four eggs. Food is chiefly insects.

Redstarts breed in holes in old trees or walls or even on buildings (sometimes in swallows' nests), and they favour the sort of country where suitable nesting sites are to be found.

This is a summer visitor in varying numbers, being absent from some areas such as Cornwall and northern Scotland. The beautiful song of this pretty member of the Thrush family is not unlike a shortened version of the Robin's*, and there is a call-note 'puweet'.

The hen builds a nest of grass, moss and roots, with a lining of hair and feathers, in which she incubates six eggs. Often there are two broods.

The food of this restless little bird consists chiefly of insects and worms, but some berries also are eaten.

*See 'Garden Birds'   38

Nightingale *(above)*
Wood Warbler *(below)*

The Nightingale is a summer visitor, not often seen but most evident through its song. It tends to hide in low cover in woods or on heaths, and in many respects is rather like a large Robin*.

The song, heard by night and day until early June, has a rapid and very loud 'jug-jug-jug' note added to a variety of phrases of great vigour and richness, particularly the single note 'piou' on an astonishing crescendo. The ordinary call-notes are harsh and croaking, and Nightingales tend to vary individually in the quality of their song.

Four or five eggs are laid in a bulky nest, on or near the ground, made of a great many dead leaves and lined with grass and hair. There is only one brood. Food consists of worms and insects with a few berries, especially elder.

Another summer visitor is the Wood Warbler, larger and more brightly coloured than the Chiff Chaff*. It prefers woodland with little or no undergrowth, and spends much time high up in big trees. However, it nests on the ground among bracken, laying six or seven eggs in a domed nest with a side entrance and lined with grass and hair, but never feathers. Food is mostly small insects.

The Wood Warbler's song has two phases – a plaintive 'whee-ou' and a long, accelerating trill 'stip-stip-sipp-sipp-sweee', during which the whole bird quivers.

*See 'Garden Birds'   40

Dartford Warbler *(above)*
Whitethroat *(below: hen left, cock right)*

The Dartford Warbler is our only resident Warbler, and is now slowly increasing in numbers after having been almost exterminated in the winter of 1947. It is found in a few places in southern England, on heaths with gorse and heather. It has a weak flight, as if its long tail were too heavy for it, and as a rule hides in cover. The song, rather like the Whitethroat's, is short and tuneful, sometimes uttered in flight and sometimes by small parties of cocks in chorus.

The nest, usually placed in heather or gorse, is built mostly by the hen, but the cock makes 'cocks' nests' like the Wren*. It is made of moss, thistledown, grass and even paper, the whole being bound together with cobwebs and spiders' cocoons. It is lined mostly with grass. There are at least two broods of four eggs. Insects and spiders form the diet.

Whitethroats are summer visitors, occurring among thick cover in a variety of places throughout Britain. Their vigorous song can be heard from April until the middle of September – 'wee-to-wee wee-tee wit-wit'. The song, sometimes uttered in dancing flight, varies considerably with individual birds.

Whitethroats nest in a bush or clump of thick grass and lay four or five eggs, usually with two broods. The nest is solidly made and sometimes built by the cock alone, although normally both parents build the nest, incubate the eggs and tend the young.

*See 'Garden Birds'   42

Redpoll (top: hen left, cock right)
Siskin (below: hen left, cock right)

These two little finches are often seen in mixed parties, particularly in winter, and are residents in various parts of Britain, but chiefly in Scotland. Both are remarkably acrobatic as they climb about, feeding on birches and alders, the seeds of which, with minute insects, provide their principal food. They are alike, too, in flight, being noticeably light and quick with a typical undulating finch action.

Redpolls nest in a variety of sites – in swamps or heather or tall trees, laying four or five eggs in a nest built by the hen. This is very roughly finished, the ends of twigs and grass being left sticking out and not bound in as with most small birds. The lining consists of white down. The young, hatched in ten or more days by the hen only, are fed by both parents. A second brood is sometimes reared.

Siskins build their nests high up in conifers and often near the end of a branch. It is a neat affair, made by the hen, of moss, lichen, grasses and twigs with a lining of wool, hair and feathers. Incubation, by the hen, takes up to twelve days and, as with Redpolls, the young fly in about fifteen days. There are two broods.

The song of both birds is twittering and high-pitched, often uttered in an elaborate display flight at breeding time. There is also the typical finch call-note – 'tseet'.

Crossbill (top: hen above, cock below)

Goldcrest (below)

Crossbills are finches, resident in the Scottish Highlands and in one district in East Anglia. Every few years large numbers arrive from the Continent in summer, spreading over most of Britain and, to a great extent, nesting here. Confined to areas where there are pine trees and plantations of larch and spruce, they feed almost exclusively on the seeds of conifers.

The tips of the Crossbill's beak are crossed over to act as an instrument for opening fir cones. The call-note is a loud 'chup-chup' and the song an odd mixture of 'chups', 'whits' and similar notes. The nest, built in a pine tree, consists of a grass and wool cup laid on a foundation of twigs. It is lined with fur and grass and usually contains four eggs.

The Goldcrest, three and a half inches long, is the smallest European bird and is resident throughout Britain. It inhabits conifer plantations and, being quite unafraid of man, will also favour gardens containing such trees as Wellingtonias. The call and song repeat a shrill, high-pitched 'zeec', ending in a trill. Food consists of insects and spiders, busily picked from the leaves of trees.

The nest is fixed, high up, to the under-side of a branch and built of moss, spiders' webs and feathers. From seven to ten minute eggs are hatched in about sixteen days. There are two broods.

Brambling *(top)*
Snow Bunting *(below: hen left, cock right)*

Both these finches are mainly winter visitors, although a few of each species occur at other times. A few Snow Buntings breed in Scotland in most years, and Bramblings have bred on a few occasions. The plumage of both birds undergoes considerable change in the breeding season, each showing much blacker than the winter plumage shown opposite.

The Brambling is rather like the Chaffinch*, in company with which it will feed, particularly in beech woods in winter when beechmast forms an important item of diet. It also feeds on other seeds and berries. The call note is 'tsweek', and 'chuc-chuc' is uttered in flight. The song is heard only at breeding time and is thus very rarely heard here.

Snow Buntings are mountain birds which are sometimes seen on the sea-shore in winter. They seldom perch on trees, spending much time on the ground, where they nest among the boulders and rocks of bare mountain tops. From four to six eggs are laid in a grassy nest lined with mixed softer material. Sometimes there are two broods.

The Snow Bunting's song is loud and musical, but short, unlike the hoarse notes of most buntings. The flight-note is 'tirr-irririp', often heard from a flock of birds as they fly overhead looking, from below, very white and like snowflakes – another name for this bird.

Food consists of grass seeds and, in summer, insects.

Corn Bunting *(above)*
Cirl Bunting *(below; cock left, hen right)*

The Corn Bunting is a resident found in large colonies on arable and grass land, particularly near the sea. It is larger than most Buntings, and has a distinctive habit of flying with dangling legs on leaving its perch – an unusual feature in a small bird. Its song is also distinctive, a series of notes based on 'quit', repeated and accelerated until it finishes on a sound like the jangling of a bunch of keys.

As its name implies, it is a seed eater, including corn which it will steal from ricks. Its nest is mainly of grass, built low down in a hedge or among crops. Three to five eggs, hatched in about twelve days, are laid, sometimes with two broods, and the young fly as early as nine days old.

Also found near the sea, mostly in the southern counties of England, is the pretty Cirl Bunting, a resident which favours mixed downland and woodland. Somewhat similar to the Yellowhammer (*page 24*) with which it forms flocks, it can be recognised by its olive rump. It nests on or near the ground, laying three or four eggs in a grass nest which includes a lot of moss. The hen alone builds the nest, incubates the eggs and feeds the young. There are at least two broods.

The Cirl's song is a repeated rattling, but it has a characteristic flight note, 'sissi-sissi-sip'.

INDEX